STANDARD
christmas
PROGRAM BOOK

PROGRAM RESOURCES FOR A JOYFUL CELEBRATION!

Reproducible Book

Compiled by
Elaina Meyers

Standard®
P U B L I S H I N G
Bringing The Word to Life

Cincinnati, Ohio

Editorial team: Elaina Meyers, Rosemary H. Mitchell, Courtney Rice
Cover design: Brigid Naglich
Inside design: Bob Korth

Published by Standard Publishing
Cincinnati, Ohio
www.standardpub.com
Copyright © 2008 by Standard Publishing.
All rights reserved.

ISBN 978-0-7847-2134-6

CONTENTS

Dramas & Skits

MUG OF KINDNESS

by Kayleen Reusser
Kathy, a young mother with a sour view of life, receives an unexpected act of kindness from a stranger, which changes her outlook.

PEACE WHEN THERE IS NO PEACE

by Regina Golden
Erin believes there is no peace in the world. Lane shares his beliefs by showing the biblical view of peace and how it affects everyone.

THE CHRISTMAS BUFFET

by Dianne McIntosh
At the buffet table of a fancy Christmas party, Phil, a socially challenged individual, challenges those filling their plates to partake of the great gift of God's Son.

Reading

AND THE WORLD WAITED

by Sharon Lessman
This reading could be used as a responsive reading or monologue and is appropriate for any Sunday in Advent. It reminds us of how we are a people waiting in hope for God.

MUG OF KINDNESS

Kayleen Reusser

Summary: Kathy, a young mother with a sour view of life, receives an unexpected act of kindness from a stranger, which changes her outlook.

Characters:

KATHY—a young mother

TRUCK DRIVER

Setting: Scene 1 takes place in a car; Scene 2 takes place in Kathy's kitchen.

Props: wrapped baby doll, car seat, chairs set up to resemble a car with front and back seats, cell phone, coffee mug

Running Time: 10 minutes

SCENE 1

KATHY pretends to drive her car that has baby doll in back seat. She talks on cell phone while peering through the windshield.

KATHY: Oh, Jane, this weather is driving me crazy. I can hardly see to find a place to park. It's going to be crazy at home tonight too. I can hardly bear to think about it. Lindsay is getting a vaccination shot which means she'll be up all night. John might be getting laid off from his job. I've got a cold. Good grief! It couldn't be much worse.

[pretends to swerve steering wheel as if on ice] Whoa! I better let you go before I run into something. Talk to you later.

[Kathy throws the phone on the seat and veers car over to parking spot.]

KATHY: *[turns to baby in back seat]* Whew! Finally found a spot. Well, Lindsay, we made it. Let's get this over with, OK?

[KATHY exits car and gets baby out of back seat. A honk comes from offstage. KATHY looks over shoulder.]

KATHY: What is that truck honking at? *[looks around]* Oh no! He's honking at me. I parked in his delivery zone! *[groans]*

[KATHY puts baby back in car and makes motions as if starting up car and moving it to a new spot. As she starts to exit again, she looks out her side window and groans when she sees the truck driver standing beside her.]

KATHY: *Now* what does he want? *[slowly exits car]*

TRUCK DRIVER: Sorry, ma'am. I saw you had a baby back there. I would have let you have the spot if I could have found another one that was big enough for my truck.
KATHY: *[eyes him suspiciously]* Uh, that's OK.
TRUCK DRIVER: Here's something for your trouble *[hands her a coffee mug]*. Merry Christmas! *[runs off]*

[KATHY stands looking after driver. Then she lowers her eyes to the mug. Lights out.]

Scene 2

Lights dim to show it's evening. Kathy is in her kitchen. She talks excitedly on the cell phone while holding the coffee mug from the truck driver.

Kathy: It was really something, Jane. I had taken that man's parking spot and yet he gave me a gift. I was speechless, and you know how hard that is to accomplish! *[laughs]* You know, it made me think about how God gave us baby Jesus. He didn't have to do it and we certainly didn't deserve it. But like John 3:16 says, He did it because He loves us. *[pause]* Yeah, it is pretty amazing. I have to go. Just wanted to share my great day with you.

[KATHY turns off phone and stares at cup. She smiles and looks up.]

Kathy: Thank You.

[Lights lower]

PEACE WHEN THERE IS NO PEACE

Regina Golden

Summary: Erin believes there is no peace in the world. Lane shares his beliefs by showing the biblical view of peace and how it affects everyone.

Characters:

ERIN and LANE—two friends of any age

PASTOR

MARY—teenager or young adult

JOSEPH—young adult

THREE (or more) SHEPHERDS

THREE (or more) ANGELS

NARRATOR

SIMEON—an older man

ANNA—an older woman

VOICE

GROUP OF ADULTS

MIRANDA—an older child or teenager

FOUR WOMEN—witnesses of the resurrection

Setting: a modern nook (two friends at a table) with ability to see a church's Christmas program

Props: table, Bible, dictionary, newspaper, speaker's stand, simple manger scene with blocks of wood for sitting, baby doll, Jewish menorah (can be made from poster board) with a cloth over it is placed near the manger scene so that the manger area can later become the temple, optional shepherds' crooks, spotlight

Costumes: ERIN, LANE, and NARRATOR are dressed in ordinary clothes. The PASTOR wears what he usually wears in church. The Bible-times costumes can be simple or as elaborate as your church's costume wardrobe will allow. (Shepherds should not be too neat and tidy.)

Running Time: 20 minutes (plus whatever music is added)

ERIN and LANE are seated at the table. A song about peace is being sung offstage [suggested: "Peace, Peace, Sweet Peace"].

ERIN: Do you hear that? Christians have the weirdest songs. "Peace, peace, sweet peace." I bet that song was written 150 years ago. Maybe there was peace then, but there's no peace now.

PEACE WHEN THERE IS NO PEACE

LANE: Actually, 150 years ago our country was fighting a civil war. No peace then. Brother was fighting against brother. Some families didn't know whether they were for the north or for the south. There wasn't any peace, for sure.

ERIN: What does peace really mean, anyway?

LANE: Look it up, friend. *[hands her a dictionary]*

ERIN: *[takes time to find it and then reads]* "Freedom from civil disturbance. Absence of war. Harmony in personal relationships." *[closes dictionary]* I don't know, but I don't think we have peace.

LANE: It's almost Christmas, and we hear a lot about peace—like on Christmas cards, on decorations, and stuff like that.

ERIN: I know. People do that because it's tradition, but there's no peace today. Have you read the paper or listened to the news?

LANE: *[next lines can be revised to show the latest disastrous news]* Yes, I know. It's hard to believe that people really hijacked our planes and turned them into weapons. They ran our planes into our own tall buildings. They killed people on purpose.

ERIN: So you agree. There's no peace today. Right?

LANE: Wait, now. I didn't say that. I have peace. I'm a Christian and I have peace in my heart.

ERIN: Well, you've got some explaining to do to convince me.

[Singing continues louder. During the song, ERIN is reading the paper and Lane is in deep thought.]

ERIN: OK, now listen to this: *[reads a few lines from the latest news of the day; can even be disturbing regional news]*

LANE: I know. It's sad, isn't it?

ERIN: Sad? It's more than sad. How can we have Christmas with all of this going on, and why would we want to anyway? And why do we have Christmas in the first place?

LANE: So how many questions is that—three all at once? Now which one do you really want answered?

ERIN: OK. How can we have Christmas with all of this going on?

LANE: Christmas is special. A real celebration of Christmas will help us understand peace and love. We can have peace in our hearts because of what God sent to this world. He sent us His Son, Jesus. He came as a baby, but He grew up.

ERIN: Yeah, I know that story about the baby in the manger. You think that really was Jesus and He really was God's Son?

LANE: I certainly do.

ERIN: But there's stuff in that story about peace, so we're right back where we started. I don't see any peace in the world today.

LANE: You'll see. There's a message I want you to hear. The pastor is right in the middle of telling it.

[The spotlight goes from the two on the platform over to the PASTOR who is standing on the right. The PASTOR begins as if he is in mid-sentence. When the spotlight leaves, he stops talking, also in mid-sentence.]

PASTOR: . . . and Jesus said, "Peace I leave with you; my peace I give you.

I do not give to you as the world gives. Do not let your hearts be troubled and do not be afraid." *[John 14:27]* My friends, *this* peace is available to all of us if . . .

[Spotlight leaves the PASTOR and goes back to ERIN and LANE. MARY and JOSEPH and the baby take their places at the manger scene, but there is no light on them yet.]

ERIN: Preachers are supposed to say stuff like that.

LANE: Just wait. When you know, really *know* God's love, you'll have peace in your heart too. I'm going to show you the first Christmas. Listen for the word *peace*.

[Spotlight goes to the manger scene. The THREE SHEPHERDS, who have been seated in the congregation, move into the center aisle of the church. As they talk, they are slowly moving toward the manger scene.]

SHEPHERD 1: The sheep seem calm and settled in for the night. I'm going to try to get a little sleep.

SHEPHERD 2: Fine. I'll take the first watch. It's a beautiful night.

SHEPHERD 3: I'll get a little rest too.

[The ANGEL 1 stands near the manger scene and turns to the shepherds. The spotlight goes to him.]

ANGEL 1: Wait! Don't go to sleep yet. I have a special message for you! There is good news! Today a savior has been born! You will find the baby lying in a manger.

[Other ANGELS join in, sharing the spotlight.]

ANGEL 2: Glory to God in the highest!

ANGEL 3: Peace! Peace on earth.

ANGEL 4: Peace among men with whom God is pleased.

[Angels leave as the spotlight moves to the shepherds.]

SHEPHERD 1: We're going to Bethlehem right now!
SHEPHERD 2: Why?
SHEPHERD 1: Because the angels said to. That's why!
SHEPHERD 2: OK, OK, I'm coming.
SHEPHERD 3: And I'm coming too. Whoever heard of angels talking to shepherds? It's got to be something special.

[SHEPHERDS move up toward the manger scene and the spotlight follows them, resting on the manger scene. As they go, someone sings, "O Come, All Ye Faithful." SHEPHERDS talk quietly to MARY and JOSEPH, and they look at the baby. "Silent Night" is sung while the shepherds are still looking at the baby. The shepherds appear to make small talk with MARY and JOSEPH.]

SHEPHERD 1: *[as he starts back toward the congregation]* I'm going to tell everyone about this baby.
SHEPHERD 2: The baby was just where the angel told us He would be. There's something special about Him. Something special!
SHEPHERD 3: Praise God. Whoever thought we'd be the ones to see Him first?

[Spotlight goes to LANE and ERIN, who are speaking quietly with each other. They don't say anything audible until the stage work is done. The manger scene quietly dismantles. As he

leaves, Joseph removes the manger, and Mary takes the cloth off of the menorah.]

LANE: So what did you think?

ERIN: That's a sweet story, but what does that have to do with the real world?

LANE: The baby's name is Jesus, and He grew up like our kids today grow up, but He was different. He was a man, but He was also God.

ERIN: How do you know He was different?

LANE: He did miracles, and He was a special teacher. It was obvious that He really was the Son of God. The Bible tells us all about it. *[picks up the Bible; his notes can be in the Bible from now on]* John 20:31 says, "These [words] are written that you may believe that Jesus is the Christ, the Son of God." Some people knew that even when He was a baby. It was revealed to them. Now watch as the young family takes their baby to the temple to do what good Jewish families did in those days. You'll see how it was revealed to at least two people. They knew that this baby really was the Son of God.

[Spotlight goes to the menorah, indicating a Jewish temple.]

NARRATOR: Luke 2:25-27. "Now there was a man in Jerusalem called Simeon . . .

[SIMEON comes into the temple from the left. ANNA comes in from the right. She has her back to the audience and is obviously praying. She remains there during the SIMEON conversation.]

NARRATOR: *[continues]* . . . who was righteous and devout, He was waiting for the consolation of Israel, and the Holy Spirit was upon him. It had been revealed to him by the Holy Spirit that he would not die before he had seen the Lord's Christ. Moved by the Spirit, he went into the temple courts."

[MARY and JOSEPH come in with Mary holding the baby doll.]

SIMEON: May I hold the baby? *[takes the baby and holds him up a little]* Now, Lord, I am ready to die. I can die in peace because I have seen Your salvation. I have seen the salvation that You prepared in the sight of all the people. Oh, thank You, God, thank You. *[gives baby back to Mary or Joseph]* This child is appointed for special things. And a sword will pierce your own soul and thoughts from many hearts will be revealed. May the Lord be praised for ever and ever.

[Simeon leaves.]

NARRATOR: There was an 84-year-old widow named Anna who never left the temple, serving night and day with fasting and prayers.

ANNA: *[walking over to the baby]* Oh, blessed be the name of the Lord. I have seen Him—the Messiah. *[holds the baby and speaks to the congregation]* This child is the Holy One of Israel. If you are looking for redemption, this is the child who will grow up and provide our salvation. Blessed be the name of the Lord! *[gives baby back to MARY or JOSEPH.]*

NARRATOR: Luke 2:39. "When Joseph and Mary had done everything required by the Law of the Lord, they returned to

Galilee, to their own town of Nazareth. And the child grew and became strong; he was filled with wisdom; and the grace of God was upon him."

[MARY, JOSEPH, and ANNA leave the stage. Spotlight is back on ERIN and LANE.]

ERIN: Yes, I think they really thought He was special. Maybe He was . . . but no *baby* can give peace to the world. There has to be more to it than that.

LANE: Now you're getting it. The baby part was just the way God chose to give Jesus to the world. The best part is yet to come. Hold on!

ERIN: I'm holding.

LANE: Jesus said in John 14:27.

VOICE: "Peace I leave with you; my peace I give you. I do not give to you as the world gives. Do not let your hearts be troubled and do not be afraid."

ERIN: That must be the answer. I've heard that twice tonight. It's a different kind of peace. I noticed that He said that His peace is not like the peace the world gives us.

LANE: Jesus also said in John 16:33.

VOICE: "I have told you these things, so that in me you may have peace. In this world you will have trouble. But take heart! I have overcome the world."

ERIN: He says, "In this world you will have trouble."

LANE: And that's true. Right? What we have now is trouble.

ERIN: So peace is something special from God that the world doesn't understand.

LANE: That's right. The kind of peace I'm talking about

is something special from God that the world doesn't understand.

ERIN: But all of this was 2,000 years ago. How does that apply to me today? Just because a good man lived a long time ago and promoted peace—well, a lot of people have done that.

LANE: But this man was God *and* man and He died for the sins of the world. He died a cruel death on the cross. His friends and disciples were devastated. Listen in.

[GROUP OF ADULTS dressed in Bible-times costumes come onstage, looking very somber. They talk softly among themselves. MIRANDA is with them.]

MIRANDA: *[speaking to one of the adults]* Why did they do that? Why did they kill Jesus? *[The adult just shakes his head. MIRANDA goes to another adult.]* Why did they do that? Why did they kill Jesus? *[No answer. MIRANDA goes to another adult.]* Why did they do that? Why did they kill Jesus?

ADULT 1: I don't know, child. I don't know. Maybe someday we will understand. *[holds Miranda close and comforts her]*

ADULT 2: Is this not the worst day in the history of the world?

ADULT 3: Yes, our leader is gone. What shall we do?

ADULT 4: And they're out to get us next. It's a fearful time, I tell you.

ADULT 2: I didn't think they would really crucify Him.

ADULT 3: He told us some things about all of this, but it was hard to beli—

[GROUP OF ADULTS are interrupted by the FOUR WOMEN who come excitedly telling about going to the tomb.]

WOMAN 1: He wasn't there in the grave. He is risen. I believe it. He is risen!

WOMAN 2: I tell you the truth. We were there. The tomb was empty.

MIRANDA: I believe! He is risen!

WOMAN 3: And some men said, "Why do you seek the living among the dead?" We didn't know what to say.

MIRANDA: I know what to say. Say, "Thank You, God!"

WOMAN 4: The men told us to go and tell His disciples.

WOMAN 1: So that's what we are doing. We're telling all *[motions to cover the ones on stage and the congregation]* of you, "Jesus has risen from the dead."

MIRANDA: *[speaking with enthusiasm]* Yes, Jesus really has risen from the dead!

[As the people disperse into the congregation, someone sings a resurrection song. The women and MIRANDA are telling people in the congregation that Jesus is risen. Then they sit wherever there is a place for them. When everyone is seated, the spotlight is back on ERIN and LANE.]

LANE: After Jesus was resurrected, He appeared to the disciples and according to John the very first word He said was *peace*. In John 20:19, *[reading from the Bible]* "On the evening of that first day of the week, when the disciples were together, with the doors locked for fear of the Jews, Jesus came and stood among them and said,

VOICE: 'Peace be with you.'"

ERIN: I really *do* want that peace in my heart.

LANE: Thank God! But wait; there's more! Verse 20 of that chapter says that after He showed them His hands and His side, the disciples rejoiced. And then Jesus said to them *again,*

VOICE: "Peace be with you! As the Father has sent me, I am sending you."

LANE: *[stands and says these lines to the congregation]* And He is still sending us out today to tell the good news. I want to tell it. I want people to know there *is* peace in the world in spite of anthrax and a failing stock market. In spite of fear and distrust. In spite of misunderstandings and evil. In spite of hunger and war. There is peace. There is peace in my heart. God is good—So, so good. Let the whole world be joyful on this Christmas because God sent His Son!

[Immediately the pastor gives the benediction. All the cast mingles with the congregation shaking hands and singing "Joy to the World" or your favorite joyful Christmas greeting.]

THE CHRISTMAS BUFFET

Dianne McIntosh

Summary: At the buffet table of a fancy Christmas party, Phil, a socially challenged individual, challenges those filling their plates to partake of the great gift of God's Son.

Characters:

FEMALE VOICE—reads Scripture at beginning of drama

AMELIA—a well-dressed, upper-crust woman

PHIL—a dirty, poorly dressed man

BOB—a dinner guest

TAMILEE—Bob's wife

MARGERY—high-class lady, good friends with Miranda

MIRANDA—high-class lady, good friends with Margery

MALE VOICE—reads Scripture at end of drama

Setting: A Christmas party at the home of a wealthy family. The center of focus is a buffet table filled with food.

Props: plates, glasses, silverware, finger food, punch, punch bowl with ladle

Running Time: 12 minutes

AMELIA is standing in front of the buffet table engrossed in filling her plate and soaking up the party atmosphere. PHIL is standing next to her doing the same. She is not looking at him.

FEMALE VOICE: "He has performed mighty deeds with his arm; he has scattered those who are proud in their inmost thoughts. He has brought down rulers from their thrones, but has lifted up the humble. He has filled the hungry with good things but has sent the rich away empty." *[Luke 1:51-53]*

AMELIA: Aren't Christmas parties a delight?

PHIL: Oh yeah, and the food's good too.

AMELIA: What did you say your name was?

PHIL: Phil. I'm the token transient.

AMELIA: Isn't that nice. Oh! There's Arlianna. Wonderful gabbing with you. Have a Merry Christmas. Arlianna!

[PHIL continues eating at the buffet. BOB walks up to the buffet with two empty glasses.]

BOB: So buddy, what's your story?

PHIL: No story. I'm eating. The Pringles invited me because I make everyone feel fortunate.

BOB: No kidding.

PHIL: If I'm offending you, I could sit on the floor somewhere. Estelle told me to stay off the furniture.

BOB: Who are you?

PHIL: Name's Phil. I'm the token transient.

BOB: No fooling?

PHIL: Don't you feel better off just for havin' seen me?

BOB: Maybe . . . but . . . well . . . to be honest, you seem out of place.

PHIL: I know what you mean. Kind of an eyesore, aren't I?

BOB: Yes, something like that.

PHIL: Well that's all part of the overall effect. It's the Charles Dickens touch. The Pringles told me to come as I am so here I am. Pretty as a picture, so to speak.

[TAMILEE shouts, unseen, from another part of the room.]

TAMILEE: Bo-ob, I'm waiting for my punch!

BOB: Oh, coming Tamilee. See ya later, Phil.

[PHIL continues to eat. MARGERY and MIRANDA walk up to the buffet table.]

MARGERY: I find these Christmas parties a trifle overdone, don't you agree, Miranda?

MIRANDA: Quite so, Margery. The music is predictable, the desserts are cloying, and the guest list, present company excluded, is boring to the extreme.

MARGERY: I agree. Yet it is our lot in life to be invited to every social gathering in the county.

MIRANDA: *[deep sigh]* I have declined a few of the invitations I received this season. There is a standard one must keep.

MARGERY: Yes, of course. Our presence at any event adds a certain level of class. I fully appreciate the attempts of the socially, shall we say, limited. But like you, I graciously decline. Standards are a must.

[MIRANDA *notices* PHIL *and begins to look concerned. She motions to* MARGERY *with her head to look at him. Both women begin to stare at him with disapproval.* PHIL *glances up from shoveling the food in his mouth and notices them staring.*]

PHIL: Say, could one of you broads hand me a piece of ham? You've been blocking the meat tray for five minutes. Don't you know how these things work? Fill your plate and move on.

MARGERY: Excuse me?

PHIL: Oh, hard of hearing, are ya? Sorry. [*very loud*] I said fill your plate and move along.

[MARGERY *and* MIRANDA *stare at him wide eyed and with renewed disapproval.*]

PHIL: Maybe I need an interpreter here. You two do speak English, don't ya?

MIRANDA: Who, pray tell, are you?

PHIL: She speaks! Name's Phil. Nice to meet ya, ladies.

MARGERY: Phil what?

PHIL: Phil-up, Philip. I go by Phil cause the "up" sounds kind of uppity. I'm definitely not uppity, if you know what I mean.

MIRANDA: I think we know what you mean.

MARGERY: Why are you eating at *this* buffet table?

PHIL: Is there another buffet somewhere else? Estelle told me this was where the grub was. You mean she's got two tables going? Those Pringles sure know how to throw a holiday shindig, don't they?

MIRANDA: This "shindig," as you so quaintly put it, is an exclusive event. I cannot imagine how someone of your social standing got in here.

PHIL: I understand your concern. I'm the token transient. Estelle felt like it would add the right touch to have a filthy, socially deprived individual hanging around the buffet table.

MARGERY: What do you mean?

PHIL: Well I'm sort of here to make you look at your own rich lives and see how blessed you are. I'm the "there but for the grace of God go I" person who makes you feel good about putting a quarter into the bell ringer's bucket. Now, could you either move along or toss me some ham?

MIRANDA: I refuse to believe you are an invited guest to this highbrow social event.

PHIL: Listen, you don't have to put on airs with me. I heard you two talking. You don't think this "high-eye-brow" event is good enough for your blood. You were worried about the boring guests, and here we are having a nice lively discussion.

MARGERY: I am appalled by your presence. I find you vulgar and offensive. This discussion we are having is not "lively." It is extremely distasteful.

PHIL: Nice meeting you too. You two ladies go to church?

MIRANDA: Of course we go to church. Church is a fundamental part of a stable social order.

PHIL: Oh. Hmm. I go to church too.

MARGERY: Of course you do. *[arches brow]* Is that in order to receive a bowl of soup?

PHIL: No. I go to learn about Jesus. You ever met Him?

MIRANDA: Met Him? You must mean: have we ever heard about Him? The answer to that question is: yes, we have.

PHIL: No, I meant met Him. Meeting Him is different.

MARGERY: I fail to see the distinction. We attend church regularly and even take an active part in church functions.

PHIL: That's nice, but it isn't what I'm talking about. Here we are celebrating Christmas and everything is so pretty and perfect it makes me wonder if Jesus would fit in at all.

MIRANDA: And just why wouldn't Jesus fit in?

PHIL: I'm not sure if you know this, but Jesus was born in a stable.

MARGERY: Don't be impertinent. We know where Jesus was born.

PHIL: You ever been in one?

MARGERY: Of course not. I am a lady, and I do not step in stables.

PHIL: Well, they usually stink.

MIRANDA: Personally, I like to envision a freshly cleaned stable with golden hay and well-groomed animals as the birthplace of Jesus.

PHIL: Ain't that nice. You got any ideas who came to see Him?

MARGERY: *[triumphantly]* Shepherds, angels, and wise men.

PHIL: Shepherds stink too. You ever worked with sheep?

MARGERY: Why do you persist in being impertinent?

PHIL: It's a gift, I guess. Does that mean you ain't never been around sheep?

MIRANDA: Of course not. We are—

PHIL: I know, I know. "Ladies." You may not believe this, but I work odd jobs. I wash dishes, sweep floors, and take out the trash. I don't make much so I live a little close to the wire.

Estelle asked me to come here tonight and be myself. I see why, now. You ladies need me. See, I'm like those shepherds. I don't live in a fine house and I don't have designer clothes. I'm not upper crust. *[leans toward them conspiratorially]* You may have guessed that by now. Those shepherds were working men sleeping out under the stars. They were dirty, sheep-smelling guys who had nothing going for them socially.

MARGERY: I see why you relate to them. Of course, I relate to the wise men: wealthy, well-read, kings, bringing suitable gifts for the king.

PHIL: I had a feeling you were going to say that. I guess my point is: do you relate to Jesus? Have you met Him?

MARGERY: Is there some reason you persist on asking that ridiculous question?

PHIL: I know Jesus. He met me at a curb on 48th Street.

MIRANDA: How picturesque.

MARGERY: Was this a hallucination perchance?

PHIL: Nope. I'd just heard the Christmas story. The preacher read something out of the Bible—Luke I think. It was a song or something that Mary had said. I remembered the words. She said that God cared for her, His humble servant, and then she said that God "lifted up the humble," that "He has filled the hungry with good things but has sent the rich away empty." I really *heard* that because I was hungry.

MIRANDA: So God sounded good because you needed a meal?

PHIL: I have to admit that caught my attention, but what kept it was the rest of the story. The preacher told about shepherds and how down-to-earth they were. He said the people who studied the Scriptures, who ate well and had money, didn't receive the invitation to the stable. At least if they did they declined. Not the right type of social event. I'm sure they had standards to keep.

MARGERY: Yes, well . . .

PHIL: Anyhow, what I heard was my invitation. I was invited to the stable just the same as anybody else. As I sat on that curb, I felt Him say, "I love you, Phil. I was born for you, I lived for you, and I died for you." So He met me there, and we've been together ever since.

MIRANDA: Then why are you still dirty and poor?

PHIL: That's a good question. I think it's because that's where Jesus wants me right now. Don't be fooled by my clothing. I'm really quite well off. This is just my transient disguise.

MARGERY: Really? So this is some sort of tasteless joke?

PHIL: Not at all. But these clothes aren't me. Look a little closer, and you'll see my ancestry is as upper crust as you can get. Top drawer, really.

MIRANDA: Top drawer? Really, I don't think so.

MARGERY: What is your family name?

PHIL: I'm a child of the king.

MIRANDA: Which king?

PHIL: "The" King. If you could hear the angels right now they'd be telling you that Jesus is born. That His light is shining. Jesus is among us. We are living in the light of our Savior. It's good news! Don't be one of the rich who walks away hungry; dig in.

MARGERY: I told you we attend church. What more do you think we need?

PHIL: Faith in God. Faith that Jesus was born, lived, and died for you. Faith is the start of humility. If you could have faith then you'd begin. You have to have faith to meet Jesus.

MIRANDA: Faith? Right here in the buffet line at the Pringles' Christmas party? I like to keep church *at* church.

PHIL: That isn't meeting Jesus. That isn't faith. That's a nice social event you call "church." Have some faith in Christmas. Believe the story. Come to God hungry and let *Him* fill you with good things.

MIRANDA: I really don't know what to say. You seem awfully eloquent for someone living "close to the wire." Are you certain you aren't some eccentric millionaire relative of Estelle's? That would make sense.

MARGERY: Yes, that would make sense. I think perhaps we are being duped.

PHIL: I am exactly who I appear to be. I am a person who lives a life completely different from yours, yet I am a child of God. I am just as important to God as you are. You are just as important to God as I am. Jesus is here ready to meet you. Don't miss this chance.

[AMELIA comes rushing up to the buffet table.]

AMELIA: Oh. *[looking at PHIL]* You're still here?

PHIL: Surprise!

AMELIA: *[latches onto the two ladies]* Margery! Miranda! So good to see you. How have you two been? I just met the most interesting man. I think he's in oil. He's so distinguished-looking and such a gentleman. You simply must meet him.

MARGERY: We would be delighted to meet a gentleman.

AMELIA: Hurry, come on then, I don't want him to get away.

[AMELIA, MARGERY, and MIRANDA move away from the table.]

PHIL: *[speaks sadly to their backs as they leave]* No, you don't want him to get away.

[lights dim]

MALE VOICE: "Here I am! I stand at the door and knock. If anyone hears my voice and opens the door, I will come in and eat with him, and he with me." *[Revelation 3:20]*

AND THE WORLD WAITED

Sharon Lessman

Summary: This reading could be used as a responsive reading or monologue and is appropriate for any Sunday in Advent. It reminds us of how we are a people waiting in hope for God.

LEADER: In the beginning was darkness,
RESPONSE: And the world waited for light and life.

LEADER: Men and women chose the darkness over the light,
RESPONSE: And the world waited for forgiveness.

LEADER: God called a people unto himself,
RESPONSE: And the world waited for the promise.

LEADER: On a night when all was dark and still,
RESPONSE: The world waited for the birth of a child.

LEADER: Jesus came healing and teaching,
RESPONSE: And the world waited for a king.

LEADER: The Savior died and was buried,
RESPONSE: And the world waited for a glimmer of light.

LEADER: Jesus arose to life and to His Father,
RESPONSE: And the world waited for the coming of the Spirit.

LEADER: The news of Jesus' life, death, and resurrection
spread throughout the world,
RESPONSE: And the world waited for the Word.

LEADER: Jesus has promised He will return in power and glory,
RESPONSE: And the world waits in joyful expectation.

POEMS

Christmas Reflections

Diana C. Derringer

The fires are burning brightly.
The candles are aglow.
The lights draped around the trees
reflect upon the falling snow.

The church choirs all are singing
of that most blessed event.
We focus our attention on the
Messiah who was sent.

As Christmas Day is nearing
we think of what it means,
the birth of baby Jesus
to suffer for our sins.

We worship and are grateful.
Please join us in our praise.
We'll thank God for His love
and for the Savior of our days.

The Wondrous Gift
Lois Rotz

One starry night in Bethlehem's town
a wondrous gift was given
to all the world, for God, in love,
sent down His Son from Heaven.
He came not as a mighty king
but as a baby small
with peace on earth, goodwill to men,
to save us one and all.

A Taste of Christmas
Douglas Raymond Rose

I love the Taste of Christmas,
the delicious day that's really rare—
with peppermint sticks for me to lick
and juicy oranges, apples, and pears.

I love the Taste of Christmas,
ginger cookies cooling on silver trays
with festive pine trees and pies to see
—All offering up their rich bouquet.

The Spirit of Christmas calls me
to honor the pure things I should—
I love the Christ of Christmas—
O Taste and see that He is good!

True Christmas
Susan Sundwall

Once, in midnight's star filled glory
rang through the heavens a wondrous story
to earth and its people waiting so long.
Bright angels revealed with their eternal song.

The ancient desire in all of creation
for a Savior of promise, born to each nation.
With "Glory to God in the highest," they said,
go shepherds and find Him, a manger His bed.

They came to the stable in Bethlehem's street,
those men of the hillside, sweet Jesus to greet.
In awe they beheld Him with Mary so mild,
the Lord who came down in the form of a child,
and bowing down humbly, bending their knee
they worshiped the one who would set us all free.

Like them, we remember the only true reason
and celebrate happily all through this season.
When gently He nears us, this small baby boy
We see the true Christmas of hope, love, and joy.

The Lowliest Creature

Pamela Kessler

His cry pierced the silence from a stable
where lowly creatures were kept.
A young mother cradled Him closely
while He and the animals slept.

A donkey gently raised his head;
and a dove softly cooed.
The Savior baby wriggled some,
as a cow, settling in, mooed.

A bright star from the sky
filtered in that dark place,
and a soft glow fell
on the sweet baby's face.

A lanky cat crouched down.
A scruffy dog came and sat
near the man by the baby.
He gave the dog's head a pat.

There were chickens pecking
for bugs in the hay.
The bats hanging high above
decided not to stay.

There were many lowly creatures
in the stable that blessed night.
But the lowliest creature there
was not found in their sight.

For the lowliest creature there that night
was not an animal, you see.
The shadow cast from the star's bright light
was from none other than me.

It was my lowly sin
that brought the babe to this place;
to save me and all mankind
through His holy love and grace.

Thank You, Lord Jesus,
for your humble, stable birth.
You showed how much You love me
and how much You think I'm worth.

The Majesty of Christmas
Lorena E. Worlein

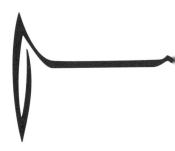

M is for the manger where the Christ child lay
sheltered in a stable sleeping on the hay.

A is for the angels heralding His birth.
"Glory in the highest, peace to men on earth."

J of course is Jesus, Savior, Lord, and King.
God's great gift from Heaven. Let His praises ring.

E is for excitement buzzing in the air.
What a wondrous message! Nothing could compare.

S is for shepherds keeping watch by night,
filled with awe and wonder at the glorious sight.

T is for the wise men traveling from afar,
bringing gifts of worship, following a star.

Y is you and me, friend. O that we might be
filled with joy and gladness at God's majesty.

Still, Still Night

Susan Sundwall

Someone comforts a baby
born in the still, still night.
Someone lies in a manger
beneath a new star's light.

Someone keeps a vigil,
guardian strong and good,
there with oxen and cattle
lowly creatures of God.

Angels 'round them hov'ring
close in the still, still night.
Shepherds tremble and wonder,
fall on their knees at the sight.

Emperors, queens, and princes
in every age to come
will bow to pay Him homage,
God's holy, chosen Son.

And yet a tender moment
before He owns our plight.
Someone comforts a baby
born in the still . . . still . . . night.

Christmas Is Forever

Lorena E. Worlein

Christmas is forever
when Christ is in the heart.
He walks along beside us
never to depart.
He left his home in Heaven,
His royal throne above,
to bring us God's glory,
His mercy and His love.

Christmas is forever
when Jesus is our Lord,
when hearts bow down before Him
and His name is adored.
All glory, laud, and honor,
all love to Him belong.
He fills our hearts with gladness
and gives to us a song.

Christmas is forever
When Christ alone is King.
"Glory in the Highest"
the courts of Heaven ring.
Jesus never changes.
Each day He is the same.
Christmas is forever.
Praise His holy name!

Christmas Is . . .

Douglas Raymond Rose

Christmas is . . .
tenderness for the past,
to our heritage holding fast,
treasuring rich memories that will last.

Christmas is . . .
courage for the present sighs,
trusting our faithful God on high—
a time to bravely do or die.

Christmas is . . .
hope for our future goals,
winning to Christ lost souls,
gathering lost sheep into His fold.

MERRY CHRISTMAS!

Christmas All Year 'Round

Douglas Raymond Rose

Hold fast to the spirit of Christmas.
It's deep in your heart that it's found;
live week by week in this special Spirit—
and it will be Christmas year 'round.

Hold true to the spirit of Christmas.
By its boundaries pledge to be bound.
If you can live it one week at a time—
it will be Christmas all year 'round.

Hold on to the spirit of Christmas.
Let genuine generosity in you be found;
live week by week in this spirit of Christmas—
and it will be Christmas all year 'round!

A Christmas Greeting
Douglas Raymond Rose

Mary had a baby boy,
'tis plain for all to see;
this Christ child in the manger
was born for you and me.

Mary had a baby boy,
the story so old—yet true.
A chant so sweet—our hearts it greets,
Merry Christmas to both me and you.

A Christmas Miracle
Douglas Raymond Rose

Unwrap the miracle of Christmas.
Unwrap it for all to see—
the miracle of Christmas
is that God loves you and me.

Unravel the great gospel ribbon.
It's the best gift under the tree—
the real miracle of Christmas
is that Christ loves you and me.

Sing We Now of Christmas

Douglas Raymond Rose

Sing we now of Christmas
reaffirming our Savior's birth;
celebrating the Christmas story
proclaiming Christ came down to earth.

Sing we now of Christmas
erasing all prejudice and pride—
God sent His Son, a sign of His love,
to live deep in our hearts and abide.

Christmas Chorus

Douglas Raymond Rose

Hear the Christmas chorus
ringing throughout the earth,
angels announcing the arrival
of our sweet Savior's birth.

Hear the Christmas chorus:
Glory to God—goodwill to men,
and the best news this Christmas
is that Jesus is coming back again!

Thank you for using this program book. To serve you better, we would like to know what you think of it. We invite you to fill out this evaluation and mail, fax, or e-mail your comments to us. We truly appreciate your time and help!

Standard Publishing, Attn: Program Book Editor, 8805 Governor's Hill Drive, Suite 400, Cincinnati, OH 45249, 513-931-0950 (fax), Christmas@standardpub.com (e-mail)

As a whole, this program book was
❏ very helpful   ❏ OK   ❏ not helpful

I would like to see more   ❏ dramas   ❏ skits   ❏ plays   ❏ poems
    ❏ readings   ❏ readers' theater   ❏ monologues
    ❏ programs   ❏ ideas for services   ❏ other:

I would like to see fewer   ❏ dramas   ❏ skits   ❏ plays   ❏ poems
    ❏ readings   ❏ readers' theater   ❏ monologues
    ❏ programs   ❏ ideas for services   ❏ other:

Please tell us why you bought this book.

What improvements or changes would you suggest for this book?

Would you like Standard Publishing to offer drama resources   ❏ for children?
    ❏ for teens?   ❏ that are topical?
    ❏ for other holidays and seasons?   ❏ other:

Do you prefer: ❏ to purchase and download drama resources from a Web site?
    ❏ to purchase drama resources in print form?

Other comments:

May we use your comments in our advertising materials?   ❏ Yes   ❏ No

Personal Info   **Church Info**
Name _____   Name of Church _____
Address _____   Address _____
City, State, Zip _____   City, State, Zip _____
Phone # _____   Church phone # _____
E-mail address _____   Church denomination and size_____

Gender: ❏ Female   ❏ Male

Age: ❏ 18–24   ❏ 25–34   ❏ 35–44   ❏ 45–54   ❏ 55+

May we contact you through mail or e-mail?   ❏ Yes   ❏ No

If you would like to write for Standard Publishing's program books, please visit www.standardpub.com and read our writer's guidelines.

.

STANDARD
christmas
PROGRAM BOOK

- Poems, plays, and programs
- Roles for children, teens, and adults
- Easy to use

All new!
Entirely reproducible!

Also available:

Christmas Programs for Children (08608)
Christmas Programs for the Church (08628)

RELIGION / Christian Ministry / General

ISBN 978-0-7847-2134-6

9 780784 721346

08658   All Ages

SECONDARY IMPACT

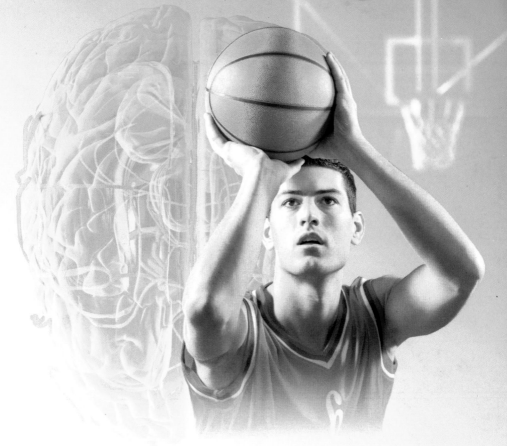

A Dr. Danny Tilson Novel
Barbara Ebel
USA TODAY BESTSELLING AUTHOR